Fantasy & Medieval Mosaics

For the Scroll Saw

by Frank Droege

Fox
Chapel Publishing Co. Inc.

1970 Broad Street • East Petersburg, PA 17520 • www.foxchapelpublishing.com

Fantasy & Medieval Mosaics for the Scroll Saw is a brand new work, first published in 2003 by Fox Chapel Publishing Company, Inc. The patterns contained herein are copyrighted by the author. Artists purchasing this book may make any number of projects based on the patterns in this book for personal use; however, mass duplication for commercial purposes is strictly forbidden. The patterns themselves may be photocopied by the artist for his or her use in making the projects, but they are not to be duplicated for resale or distribution under any circumstances.

Publisher	Alan Giagnocavo
Book Editor	Ayleen Stellhorn
Cover Design	Tim Mize
Desktop Specialist	Linda Eberly

ISBN 1–56523–199–6
Library of Congress Preassigned Card Number: 2003106768

To order your copy of this book,
please send check or money order
plus $3.50 shipping to
Fox Books
1970 Broad Street
East Petersburg, PA 17520

Or visit us on the web at
www.foxchapelpublishing.com

Printed in China
10 9 8 7 6 5 4 3 2 1

Because scrolling wood and other materials inherently includes the risk of injury and damage, this book cannot guarantee that creating the projects in this book is safe for everyone. For this reason, this book is sold without warranties or guarantees of any kind, expressed or implied, and the publisher and author disclaim any liability for any injuries, losses or damages caused in any way by the content of this book or the reader's use of the tools needed to complete the projects presented here. The publisher and the author urge all scrollers to thoroughly review each project and to understand the use of all tools involved before beginning any project.

Table of Contents

About the Author

Designing scroll saw mosaic patterns and pieces can be described as a passionate pastime for Frank Droege. His first love is painting, however, and over the years he has won numerous awards as a traditional painter. Frank studied under George Vail from the Haddonfield Art League and Max Gottlieb at the Fleisher Art Memorial in Philadelphia, Pennsylvania. He currently paints miniature art and has recently become an award-winning artist in the field.

Frank lives in Voorhees, New Jersey, with his wife and daughters. Inquiries about his artwork can be addressed directly to Frank at 306 Kresson-Gibbsboro Road, Voorhees, NJ 08043.

Creating a Scroll Saw Mosaic

Scroll saw mosaics are a variation on scroll saw segmentation techniques. To create a scroll saw mosaic, the pattern is cut apart, each piece is sanded and colored, and then the pieces are reassembled. The technique is similar to the mosaics of ancient Rome, in which elaborate scenes were created from broken pieces of colored tile.

Basic Cutting Techniques

Mosaics are simple and fun to create. Simply saw the pattern pieces, round the edges and glue the pieces back together on a ⅛ in. backing. The rounded corners give the finished artwork the illusion of ceramic tile mosaics.

Because the wood will be colored, I recommend using softwoods, such as white pine or white cedar. A #2 scroll saw blade, reverse tooth, is ideal for cutting. The reverse tooth eliminates tear-out and reduces the number of burrs that will need to be sanded off the bottom of the piece.

To round the corners of the cut pieces, I use a hand-held grinder or micro-motor tool fitted with a

Segmentation at a Glance

Illustration 1

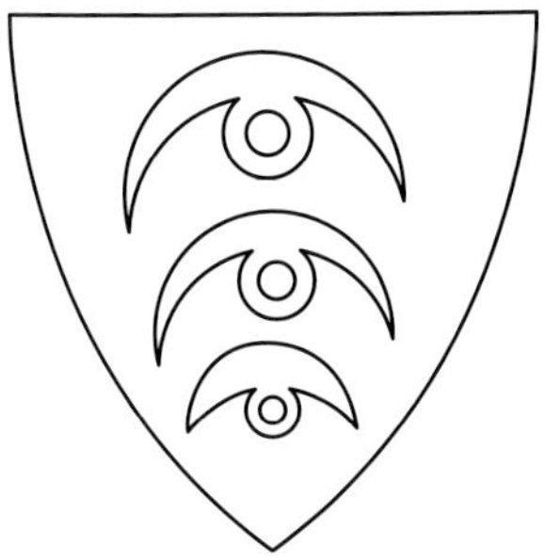

The scene or figure is cut from ⅜ in. wood according to the pattern.

Illustration 2

The edges of each piece are rounded, and the pieces are colored.

Illustration 3

The rounded, colored pieces are assembled and glued to a ⅛ in. backing.

¼ in. sanding band. You may also choose to use a hand sander. Round the corners of each piece to a uniform ⅟₃₂–⅟₁₆ in. radius.

When the pieces are rounded to your satisfaction, stain or paint each piece according to the suggested color scheme or with colors of your choosing. For the patterns in this book, I used a variety of commonly available wood-toned stains to give the pine or cedar the look of exotic woods. You could also either use brightly colored acrylic paints on all the pieces to duplicate the look of a tile mosaic, or paint only selected pieces to form an interesting final piece.

Allow the pieces to dry; then glue the pieces to the backing with yellow wood glue. Create any additional fine details, such as stonework, feathers and dragon scales, with paint or a woodburner; then finish the entire piece with acrylic varnish. Hang the piece for display with saw-tooth hooks or wire-and-eye hooks.

Remember, you can simplify any piece by removing lines and decreasing the number of pieces in any pattern.

- **Step One:** Cut two pieces of wood a little larger than the pattern you wish to scroll: a ⅛ in.-thick piece for the backer and a ⅜ in.-thick piece for the pattern.

- **Step Two:** Glue the pattern to the ⅜ in. board with rubber cement. Number each part of the pattern for easier assembly later.

- **Step Three:** Saw the frame first; then saw the remaining pieces.

- **Step Four:** Remove all the burrs from the backs of the pieces with sandpaper.

- **Step Five:** Transfer the numbers you wrote on the pattern to the bottom of each piece; then carefully pull the paper pattern off the wood.

- **Step Six:** Assemble—but don't glue—the pieces inside the frame; then sand the top of the entire project with 220-grit sandpaper.

- **Step Seven:** Remove the pieces from the frame and round the edges of each piece, including the frame, to about a ⅟₃₂ in.-⅟₁₆ in. radius. Leave the outer edge of the frame square. (Tip: Writing the numbers on the backing will make the final assembly much easier.)

- **Step Eight:** Use a tack cloth to remove any saw dust from the pieces; then paint the sides and edges of each piece according to the color plan.

- **Step Nine:** Glue the frame to the backing. Starting with a corner piece, carefully assemble and glue the pieces in the frame. Add any fine details.

- **Step Ten:** When the glue has dried according to the manufacturer's directions, apply a satin varnish to the entire piece.

Staining Mosaic Pieces

Staining is a great way to add the look of exotic hardwoods to your finished mosaic. Medieval mosaics, featuring knights, castles and coats of arms, are a perfect subject on which to experiment with stains.

I suggest that you use water-based stains. Water-based stains, such as Minwax™ and Zip Guard™, penetrate the wood quickly and are easy to clean up. Most stains are named according to their natural wood counterpart.

Choose your colors; then cut the pattern according to the directions, stopping after Step Six (trial assembly). Pull the pieces from the pattern, arranging them in piles according to color. I usually start to pull pieces from the design beginning with those to which I want to apply light-colored stains. I then move on to the middle tones, and finally to the darker tones. I always stack each color in front of a can of stain so that I don't mix up the colors. Round each piece as instructed in Step Seven, being sure to put the pieces back in the correct piles. You are now ready to stain.

Stain each piece according to the manufacturer's directions. Pay careful attention to the manufacturer's recommendations for ventilation and disposal. When applying stains, make sure you color not only the tops and rounded edges of the piece, but also a little bit of the sides. If you neglect to do this, chances are that some of the natural wood will show on your finished project. Do not stain the bottoms of the pieces.

The staining chart provided on the can by the manufacturer will show the different intensities of color. Remember that the color of the stain also depends on the wood you use. All of the projects in this book began as white cedar or white pine. To get a white stain, dilute some white acrylic paint, apply it to the piece, then rub it off with a cloth.

Allow the pieces to dry completely before finishing the mosaic as instructed on the previous page.

A variety of stains applied to the segmented pieces of the pattern creates the illusion of more expensive hardwoods. This piece was cut from ⅜" pine.

© Frank Droege

© Frank Droege

© Frank Droege

Knight's Shield

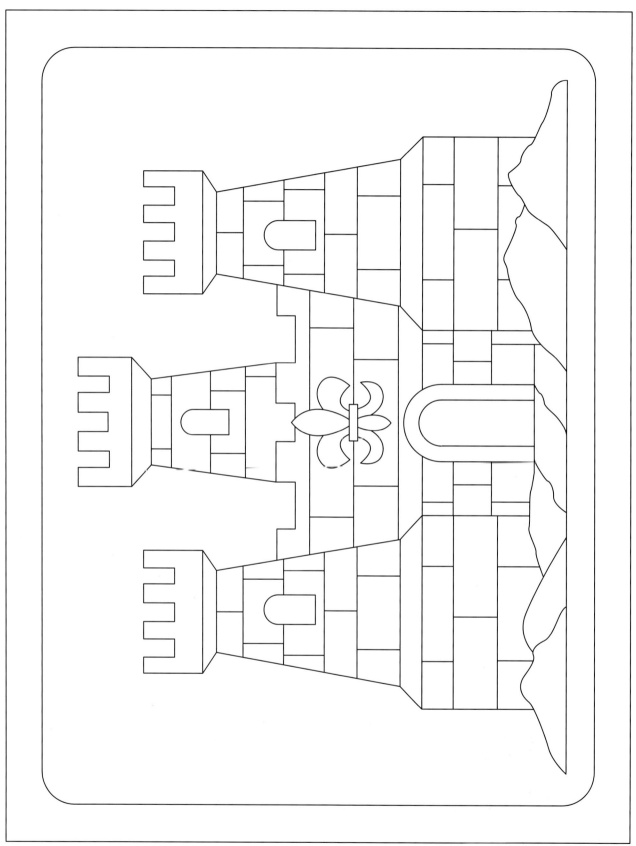

© Frank Droege

Castle Fleur de Lis

© Frank Droege

Cathedral Fortress

© Frank Droege

Dragon Protector

Winged Guardian

© Frank Droege

© Frank Droege

Serpent King

© Frank Droege

© Frank Droege

© Frank Droege

River Fortress

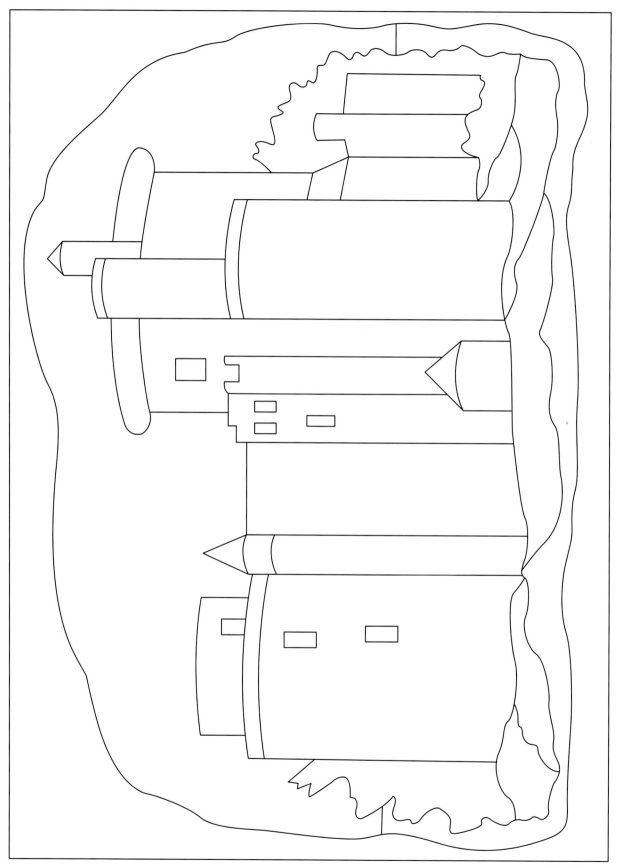

© Frank Droege

Forest Stronghold

© Frank Droege

Shadow Castle

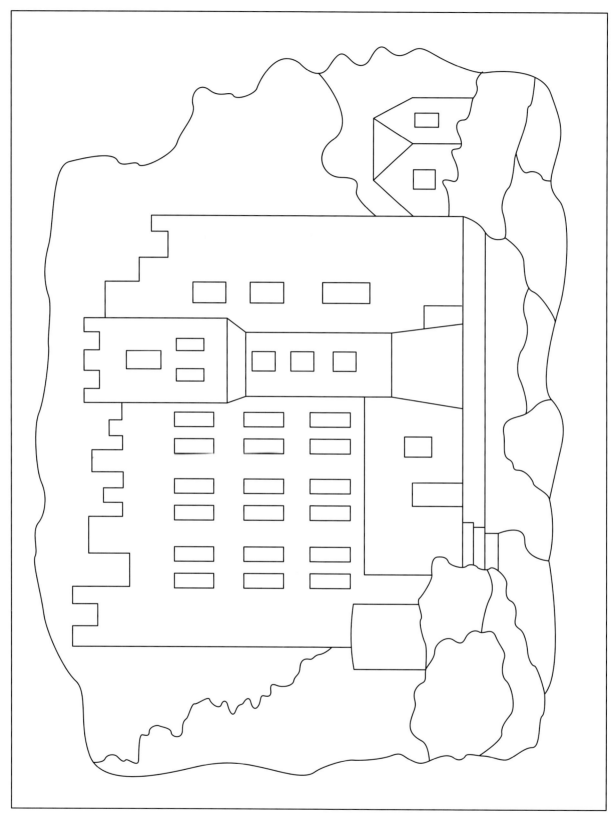

© Frank Droege

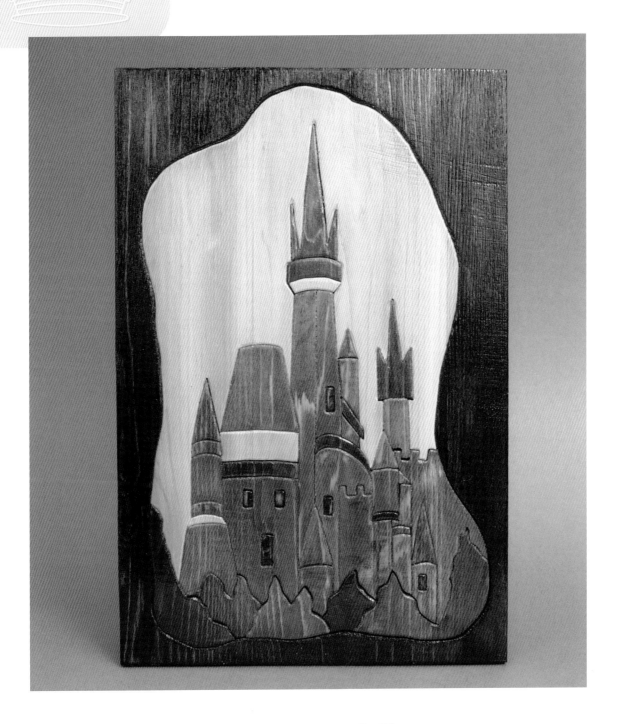

Unicorn Palace

© Frank Droege

Watchful Eye

© Frank Droege

Castle Shield

Scroll Saw
Fantasy & Medieval Mosaics

Valiant Knight

© Frank Droege

Defender's Shield

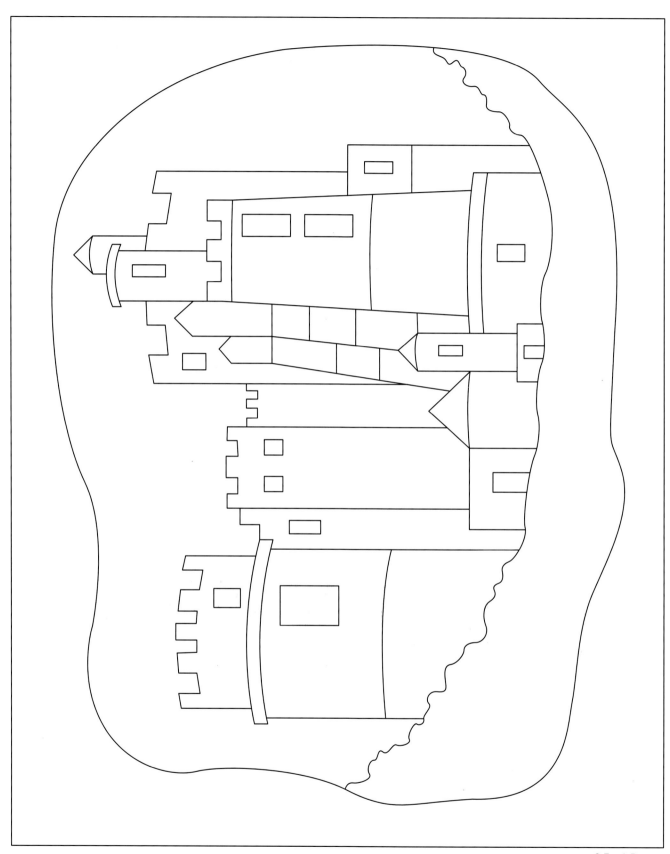

© Frank Droege

© Frank Droege

© Frank Droege

© Frank Droege

Painted Mosaics

Mosaics can also be painted for a completely different effect. Use acrylic paints and paint each piece separately after sanding. Paint the tops of the pieces and half-way down the sides. Do not paint the bottoms of the pieces.

Castle Guard, pattern on page 38

Heraldic Champion, pattern on page 62

Castle Shield, pattern on page 48

Painted Mosaics

Valiant Knight, pattern on page 50

More Great Project Books from Fox Chapel Publishing

- **Country Mosaics for Scrollers and Crafters by Frank Droege:** Bless your friends, neighbors and even your own home with these wooden plaques symbolizing faith, love, and prosperity! Over 30 patterns for hexsigns, marriage blessings, house blessings and more included.
ISBN: 1-56523-179-1, 72 pages, soft cover, $12.95.

- **Scroll Saw Mosaics by Frank Droege:** Use these 30 easy-to-cut segmentation patterns to create colorful wooden mosaics. Basic cutting techniques and shop-tested outline patterns for each design included. Use his color suggestions or make your own color combinations for eye-catching works of art.
ISBN: 1-56523-160-0, 64 pages, soft cover, $9.95.

- **Great Book of Dragon Patterns by Lora S. Irish:** Guide for creating your own fantastic renderings of man's favorite foe-the dragon! Use the author's patterns or apply her techniques to create your own. Includes 72 patterns, basic dragon anatomy, fascinating dragon lore, evolution and more!
ISBN: 1-56523-155-4, 144 pages, soft cover, $19.95.

- **Intarsia Workbook by Judy Gale Roberts:** Learn the art of intarsia from the #1 expert, Judy Gale Roberts! You'll be amazed at the beautiful pictures you can create when you learn to combine different colors and textures of wood to make raised 3-D images. Features 7 projects and expert instruction. Great for beginners!
ISBN: 1-56523-226-7, 72 pages, soft cover, $14.95.

- **Scroll Saw Holiday Puzzles by Tony and June Burns:** Celebrate the holidays with these adorable wooden puzzles. You'll find ready-to-use patterns for 30 projects including nativity scene, leprechaun, pumpkin, menorah, birthday cake, Santa Claus and more. Cutting and staining instructions included.
ISBN: 1-56523-204-6, 72 pages, soft cover, $14.95.

- **Wooden Chess Sets You Can Make by Diana Thompson:** Handcraft a classic or contemporary chess set that will be cherished for years to come. You will learn to create each piece by using compound cuts on the scroll saw. Patterns and full-color photographs for each of the playing pieces (king, queen, bishop, knight, rook, pawn) are included. Instructions and pattern for a beautiful inlay playing board also included.
ISBN: 1-56523-188-0, 72 pages, soft cover, $14.95.

Call 800-457-9112 or visit us on the web at www.foxchapelpublishing.com to order!

Scroll Saw WorkShop
The How-To Magazine for Scrollers

Don't Miss A Single Issue - Subscribe Today!

Each full color issue will contain:

- **Detailed illustrations & diagrams**
- **Ready-to-use patterns**
- **Step-by-step instructions**
- **Crisp, clear photography**
- **Must have tips for beginners**
- **Challenging projects for more advanced scrollers**
- **Interviews with leading scrollers, and more...**

All to help you become the best scroller you can be!

50 EASY WEEKEND SCROLL SAW PROJECTS
By John A. Nelson

FREE with a 2-year paid subscription!
58 Pages, 8.5 x 11 soft cover
$10 value!

Includes:
- *50 simple, useful projects*
- *Easy-to-understand patterns*
- *Practical pieces, including clocks, shelves, plaques and frames*